Science Questions

How Do Rainbows Form?

by Rebecca Pettiford

Bullfrog
Books

Ideas for Parents and Teachers

Bullfrog Books let children practice reading informational text at the earliest reading levels. Repetition, familiar words, and photo labels support early readers.

Before Reading

- Discuss the cover photo. What does it tell them?

- Look at the picture glossary together. Read and discuss the words.

Read the Book

- "Walk" through the book and look at the photos. Let the child ask questions. Point out the photo labels.

- Read the book to the child, or have him or her read independently.

After Reading

- Prompt the child to think more. Ask: Have you ever seen a rainbow? Where was it?

Bullfrog Books are published by Jump!
5357 Penn Avenue South
Minneapolis, MN 55419
www.jumplibrary.com

Library of Congress Cataloging-in-Publication Data

Names: Pettiford, Rebecca, author.
Title: How do rainbows form? / by Rebecca Pettiford.
Description: Minneapolis, MN: Jump!, Inc., [2023]
Series: Science questions | Includes index.
Audience: Ages 5–8
Identifiers: LCCN 2022011599 (print)
LCCN 2022011600 (ebook)
ISBN 9798885240505 (hardcover)
ISBN 9798885240512 (paperback)
ISBN 9798885240529 (ebook)
Subjects: LCSH: Rainbows—Juvenile literature.
Classification: LCC QC976.R2 P48 2023 (print)
LCC QC976.R2 (ebook)
DDC 551.56/7—dc23/eng20220503
LC record available at
https://lccn.loc.gov/2022011599
LC ebook record available at
https://lccn.loc.gov/2022011600

Editor: Jenna Gleisner
Designer: Emma Bersie

Photo Credits: S.Borisov/Shutterstock, cover; AmazingPixels/Shutterstock, 1; Blacqbook/Shutterstock, 3; Dmitry Shishkin/Dreamstime, 4; Denis Belitsky/Shutterstock, 5, 23tr; H. Mark Weidman Photography/Alamy, 6–7, 23tl; Valentinka.ph/Shutterstock, 8–9; Radomir Rezny/Shutterstock, 10; Sakkarin Kamutsri/Dreamstime, 11; Zaitsava Olga/Shutterstock, 12–13tl; Iakov Kalinin/Shutterstock, 12–13tr; Viktor Pecheroga/Shutterstock, 12–13b; noisuk Photo/Shutterstock, 14, 23bl; yanikap/iStock, 15; Cn Boon/Alamy, 16–17, 23br; Olha Rohulya/Alamy, 18–19; Sergiy Bykhunenko/Shutterstock, 20–21; Eladora/Shutterstock, 22; merrymuuu/Shutterstock, 24.

Printed in the United States of America at Corporate Graphics in North Mankato, Minnesota.

Table of Contents

Seven Colors

The rain stops.

The clouds clear.
The Sun shines.

Look!

It is a rainbow!

It is an arc.

We see a rainbow.
But we can't touch it.
Why?
It is made of light!

We see rainbows
after it rains.

We also see them by waterfalls.

waterfall

water

sunlight

rainbow

Why?

They need water and sunlight to form.

A waterdrop acts like a prism.

prism

Sunlight hits the drops.

The light bends.

It breaks up into colors.

15

We see a spectrum.
It has seven colors.
What colors
do we see?

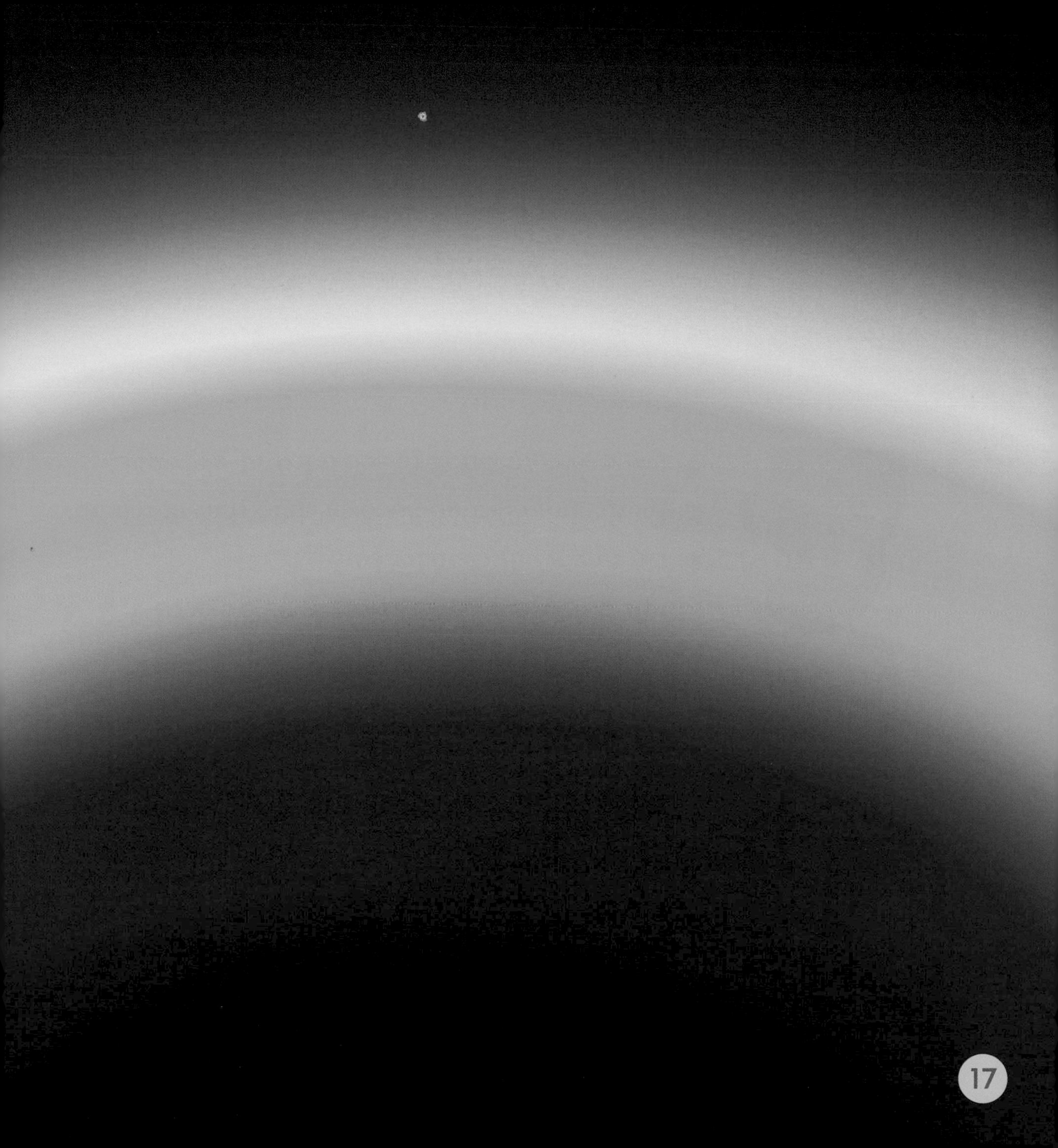

Look!

We see two rainbows!

Rainbows are beautiful!

Have you seen one?

How a Rainbow Forms

Rainbows form when sunlight hits waterdrops. To see a rainbow, the Sun has to be behind us. Waterdrops have to be in front of us. Take a look!

Picture Glossary

arc
Part of a curve, or a half circle.

clear
To make or become bright.

prism
A clear, solid glass shape that breaks up light into the colors of the spectrum.

spectrum
The bands of color that show when light shines through a prism or drops of water.

Index

To Learn More

Finding more information is as easy as 1, 2, 3.

❶ Go to www.factsurfer.com

❷ Enter "howdorainbowsform" into the search box.

❸ Choose your book to see a list of websites.